COLORADO TROLLEYS

A Quick History

of

Colorado's Streetcar Lines

by

Leland Feitz

Published by
LITTLE LONDON PRESS
716 E. Washington St.
Colorado Springs, Colorado

COLORADO TROLLEYS

Where and When

Denver
1871-1950

Pueblo
1879-1948

Colorado Springs
1887-1932

Cripple Creek
1897-1922

Greeley
1910-1923

Ft. Collins
1907-1952

Boulder
1899-1931

Trinidad
1904-1926

Grand Junction
1890-1928

Durango
1883-1920

Leadville
Aspen

Horsecars on lower Seventeenth Street. The towered building at the end of the street was the union station. (Denver Public Library Western Collection)

Denver's horsecar barns were at Seventeenth and Wynkoop. (State Historical Society of Colorado)

4

DENVER

While additional lines were built and while any number of changes were made along the already established lines, Denver's basic transit system was pretty well established by 1900. Up until then more than forty companies had been formed to provide the Mile High City with transportation services. In time, they all consolidated into the Denver City Tramway Company, a complex system of some 156 miles of track.

The city's first transit service started with horsecars in 1871. The little cars were pulled over two miles of track from Seventh down Larimer to Sixteenth Street, along Sixteenth to Champa Street and then out it to Twenty-seventh. Meeting with the public's approval, more lines were built, and by 1884 the company boasted forty-five cars, 200 horses and more than 100 employees.

In 1886, Denver's first and the world's second electric cars went into operation on Fifteenth Street. The cars picked up their power from a slot in the street between the rails. While the system was sound in theory, it was abandoned in 1887 because of involved local problems. Horsecars returned.

A period of great rivalry in cable line construction between two companies then followed. Denver, in 1890, had one of the world's most complete cable car systems. A seven mile line was believed to have been the longest cable route in the world.

Attention about this time once again turned to the development of the electric car. The technique of picking up power from overhead wires had been refined by then, and by 1900 all the city's cable cars had been replaced with trolleys.

Early in the century, the tramway company built an interurban line from the city to the foothills, reaching Golden by way of Arvada. A second line, via Lakewood, was built to Golden in 1909.

An idea for the use of trailer cars during the rush hours was conceived in 1912 and eight years later over 120 of these Fifty-three passenger trailers were in service. An estimated 3,700 Denver University students earned their way through classes by serving as conductors.

While buses were brought into tramway service as early as 1925, streetcars continued in use in Denver until 1950. Then for still another five years, the big electric rubber-tired trolleys, introduced in 1940, continued to run on some of the city's streets.

5

Denver was served by a system of horsecars from 1871. This one operated over a mile and a quarter of track in east Denver. The team pulled the car up from Williams Street to Colorado Boulevard then boarded the trailer for the return trip. (State Historical Society of Colorado)

Many years after all of Denver's other horsecars had retired, the Cherrelyn line continued to operate in Englewood as a tourist curiosity. The horse pulled the car to the top of a South Broadway hill then rode back down. (State Historical Society of Colorado)

6

Denver's first electric cars operated on Fifteenth Street during the mid-1880's. They were soon adandoned however in favor of horse and cable cars. (State Historical Society of Colorado)

Cable car at Fifteenth and Lawrence. By 1890, Denver's cable car system was one of the most extensive in the country. One line, 65,600 feet long, was the longest cable line in the world.

The Denver Tramway's power house once stood at the corner of Colfax and Broadway. Cable cars are seen in the foreground. (State Historical Society of Colorado)

Denver's first electric car with the overhead trolley went into service on Christmas day 1889, on South Broadway. (State Historical Society of Colorado)

8

Denver City Tramway's central loop in 1906. (State Historical Society of Colo.)

When Lawrence was one of downtown Denver's busy streets, electric cars passed through it every few minutes, day and night. (State Historical Society of Colorado)

Trolley on East Colfax headed for Broadway. The big building to the right, where the May-D & F store now stands, was the city hall. The time was 1900. (Collection of Paul Garde)

Trolleys at Fifteenth and Curtis, at the turn-of-the-century. (State Historical Society of Colorado)

When Curtis Street was Denver's entertainment center, streetcars traveled its bright length. Edison called it the world's best lighted street. (Denver Public Library Western Collection)

Open air observation cars became popular in Denver as the city's fame as a tourist center spread. They operated over several routes, some running as far as Golden. The Brown Palace Hotel can be seen behind the car. (State Historical Society of Colorado)

Fresh air cars were especially popular in mile high Denver which at the turn of the century was a favorite health center. (Denver Tramway Collection)

Car number 67 returning from Golden over the first Sixteenth Street viaduct. The union station's shelter is at the right. (State Historical Society of Colorado)

Three cars on the busy East Seventeenth Avenue route. (State Historical Society of Colorado)

The Woeber Carriage Company of Denver built many of the cars used in Colorado. This Denver car sported padded rattan seats. (State Historical Society of Colorado)

Reading the overhead ads was a favorite pastime of the people who rocked to and from their destinations on streetcars. The cars had a nightly bath. (Denver Tramway Collection)

During World War I, Denver Tramway employed many women as conductors and a few as "motormen." (Denver Public Library Western Collection)

During 1919 and 1920 the Denver Tramway became involved in a bitter dispute with its workers over wages. The climax came in the summer of 1920 when rioters overturned several cars on East Colfax.

15

Denver Tramway Building and car barn between Thirteenth and Fourteenth Streets on Arapahoe. (Denver Public Library Western Collection)

Storage tracks were located on two levels of the Arapahoe barn in downtown Denver. It was the central division carhouse. (Denver Public Library Western Collection)

These were the Broadway yards of the Denver Tramway. They were at South Broadway and West Alaska Place. (Denver Tramway Collection)

The power that drove Denver's electric cars was generated in this giant plant located at Fourteenth and Platte. (Denver Tramway Collection)

17

Denver loved and used her trolleys as is evidenced by this well filled Barnum car returning to that area from downtown. The rental of advertising space for special events added to the company's income.

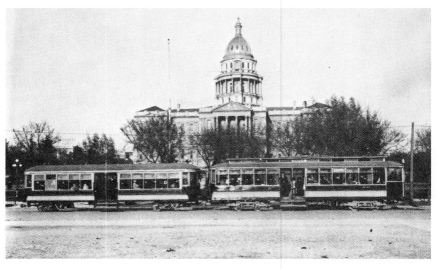

Street car and Denver-built Woeber trailer passing the Colorado state capitol building on Broadway. The gold domed building stands exactly one mile above sea level. (Denver Public Library Western Collection)

18

Car number 381 on Sixteenth at Champa just days before service ended. The old May Co. is at the right. (State Historical Society of Colorado)

In 1940 a new kind of trolley started to roll through Denver. These rubber tired trolleys provided the city with clean, quiet transportation for another five years. (State Historical Society of Colorado)

Denver's last streetcars ran on June 5, 1950. It was a sad day for many Denverites. (State Historical Society of Colorado)

It's all over. These bright yellow Denver Tramway cars are waiting to be junked. (State Historical Society of Colorado)

PUEBLO

Pueblo was only four years old when, in 1874, the city fathers first pondered a proposal for a street railway system. The city was growing by leaps and bounds, and its busy streets were either ankle deep in mud or dust. The people were demanding a public transportation system.

The Pueblo Chieftain wrote: "Give us horsecars!"

It wasn't until 1879 however that horsecar service did begin. The first line ran from Union and West B to North Santa Fe and Fifth Street, then the "hub" of Pueblo. People of the city gladly paid their ten cent fares for the slow but comfortable ride.

When the new steel mill of the Colorado Fuel & Iron Corporation went into operation, the tramway extended its narrow gauge tracks to that plant and then on to other parts of the city.

Horses continued to pull the streetcars until June 6, 1890, a date that marked a real milestone in Pueblo's progress. For that was the day the streetcar system became electric powered, and the new cars started moving through the city at the amazing speed of twelve miles an hour!

It was the second city west of the Mississippi River to adopt the new form of transportation. Pueblo, in fact, had electric cars before New York, Chicago, Washington or Boston.

Keeping pace with the rapid growth of the Steel City, the Pueblo City Railway Company continued its expansion and by the turn of the century, Puebloans could ride almost anywhere in town for only a nickel. The company operated cars over seventy-eight miles of track.

The first electric cars were small affairs, but by about 1900 large 36-passenger cars were coming into vogue. These larger cars handled the mass movement of travelers in the city until the early twenties, when the development of automobiles cut into the volume of traffic and profits. It was then that the smaller all-steel cars were put into use, first on the stub lines, and by 1930 on the main lines.

Experiments with buses began in Pueblo prior to World War II. In 1946, the first ones went into service. But it wasn't until 1948, that the transition from streetcars to buses was finally completed.

Until 1883, this giant cottonwood tree stood in the middle of Pueblo's Union Avenue, route of the city's first horsecar line. (Collection of the Southern Colorado Power Company)

Pueblo's little horsecars held twelve passengers. This car traveled from the city to the then new "steel works". (Collection of the Southern Colorado Power Company)

From the early part of the century, modern streetcars on double tracks lent a metropolitan touch to Pueblo's Main Street. (State Historical Society of Colorado)

The scene changed in a few years with the addition of new street lamps and a new form of transportation.

Pueblo's trolleys once traveled over seventy-eight miles of track. This car is pictured on the Union Avenue bridge which spans the railroad yards and the Arkansas River. (State Historical Society of Colorado)

Pueblo's streetcar system was improved in 1912 with the addition of these handsome new thirty-six passenger cars. They required a two man crew, motorman and conductor. (Collection of the Southern Colorado Power Company)

The increasing number of automobiles made operation of the large streetcars in Pueblo uneconomical so in the 1920's these smaller one-man cars were put into use. They were used until abandonment of the line in 1948. Car 123 is pictured in front of the Pueblo County Court House. (Collection of the Southern Colorado Power Company)

These were the big brick barns on South Victoria Street which housed Pueblo's streetcars. Next to them stood the Arkansas Valley Light and Power Company plant which generated the power to run the cars. (Collection of the Southern Colorado Power Company)

Colorado Springs' first electric car. It operated on Tejon Street, out as far as Stratton Park. This picture was probably taken in 1890. (Denver Public Library Western Collection)

Tejon Street car crossing Pikes Peak Avenue in the early 1890s. The original Antlers Hotel, destroyed by fire in 1898, is in the background. (Denver Public Library Western Collection)

COLORADO SPRINGS
&
MANITOU SPRINGS

Colorado Springs enjoyed the convenience of a public transportation service starting in 1887. That was the year the first horsecars went into use on Tejon Street between Costilla and Cache La Poudre Streets. The first line was soon extended farther north and another was built to Colorado City and beyond.

Electric cars replaced the horse cars in 1890, but the transit system did not grow with the town until after Cripple Creek mining king Winfield Scott Stratton bought it in 1900 for $350,000. Before he died, two years later, he had pumped over $2,000,000 into the system, making his Colorado Springs & Interurban Railway one of the finest city transportation organizations in the world.

New lines were built to reach Prospect Lake, Manitou Springs, Broadmoor, Stratton Park and Roswell. Eighty spiffy new cars ran over the systems forty-one miles of track.

The motormen were all outfitted in new blue suits. They shared with another 120 employees in the first group insurance plan sponsored by any transit company in the country. The company also helped their employees buy their own homes through a unique home loan plan.

On the day Stratton died, all the streetcars in Colorado Springs stopped running for five minutes. His investment in the city's transit system was not financially justified. Multi-millionaire Stratton just wanted his town to have the best, and he didn't care what it cost him.

After Stratton's death, the men who managed his vast estate maintained the streetcar system at the same high level. Starting about 1911, the company faced constantly decreasing traffic and it resorted to various measures to reduce expenses. First schedules were cut back. Then by 1919 all the big long cars were replaced with smaller ones which cost less to operate.

On the last day the streetcars operated in Colorado Springs, some 40,000 people turned out for a final ride. That was April 30, 1932.

While Manitou Springs was linked to its sister city by Stratton's interurban, it also had its very own trolley system from 1895 to 1928. The little line, which was only about three-quarters of a mile long, ran from the Loop in Manitou, end of the Colorado Springs line, up Ruxton Avenue to Iron Springs and the Pikes Cog Road depot.

Two cars meet at the "Busy Corner" a block from the new Antlers in this 1909 photograph. (State Historical Society of Colorado)

Car Number 52 at the Pavillion in Cheyenne Canyon's popular Stratton Park. (Western History Department, Penrose Public Library - James O. Hermansen Collection)

During the summer months, the Colorado Springs and Interurban Railway brought thousands of tourists to Manitou. When this picture was taken, soon after the turn-of-the-century, the Cliff House seen in the background was one of the West's finest resort hotels. (Denver Public Library Western Collection)

A little trolley line only about three-quarters of a mile long ran between the Loop in Manitou, the end of the Colorado Springs line, and the Pikes Peak Cog Road depot. (Denver Public Library Western Collection)

No expense was spared in building Colorado Springs' coaches. The forty-two foot cars were painted olive green, each had cherry wood doors, frosted glass and ceilings of inlaid birdseye maple. The cars seated 100 comfortably and up to 150 with some crowding. (Penrose Public Library)

During the tourist season, open cars like this one were run between Colorado Springs and Manitou, as often as every two minutes. (Denver Public Library Western Collection)

Many of the streetcars which operated in Colorado Springs were built and finished in the transit company's own car barn. (Denver Public Library Western Collection)

Studebaker sprinkler car at the foot of the West Colorado overpass. The sprinkler helped to keep the dust at a minimum and Colorado Springs clean. (Penrose Public Library)

31

The car barn for the Colorado Springs streetcars was in the 500 block of South Tejon Street. The building still stands. (Penrose Public Library)

Pikes Peak Avenue and Nevada about 1929, three years before streetcars were replaced by buses. (Denver Public Library Western Collection)

CRIPPLE CREEK & VICTOR

For about a quarter of a century, the cities and the mines of the famed Cripple Creek gold camp were joined together by the highest interurban railroad in North America. The little electric cars curved through rugged canyons and climbed over steep hills to serve almost every corner of the mining district, perched so high in the Colorado Rockies.

The first system, known as **The High Line,** came into being in 1897. The six-mile line ran between Cripple Creek and Victor via Midway and Battle Mountain, reaching an elevation of 10,487 feet near Midway. The High Line's little forty passenger cars ran on an hourly schedule until well after midnight.

In 1899, **The Low Line** was built from Cripple Creek to Victor by way of Anaconda and Elkton, and on to Goldfield and Independence. Low Line cars ran every thirty minutes day and night.

Owing to the gold camp's decline, trolley service there was greatly reduced after 1919. The trolleys stopped running altogether in 1922. By then, only 6,000 people lived in the district which had once boasted a population of over 50,000.

All the cities and many of the mines of the Cripple Creek District were connected by a complex streetcar system. This turn-of-the-century map indicates their routes. (Denver Public Library Western Collection)

Streetcars on Bennett Avenue, Cripple Creek's "main street." Electric cars passed through the city's principal streets from 1897 until 1922.

When 18,000 people lived in Victor, trolley cars rattled through the downtown section every few minutes.

Only in the Cripple Creek District could a miner ride a modern electric car directly from his own neighborhood to the gold mines where he worked. This High Line car is seen at the Portland Mine. Seven hundred men worked there.

High Line and Low Line cars made frequent runs throughout the gold camp, day and night. The fare was only five cents. (Denver Public Library Western Collection)

Double tracks ran through downtown Greeley along Eighth Avenue, the towns main street. The old Camfield Hotel can be seen at the right. (Greeley Municipal Museum)

Seventh Street and Twelfth Avenue, Greeley, Colo.

Two of the first street cars to serve Greeley meet at the corner of Seventh Street and Twelfth Avenue. (Greeley Municipal Museum)

GREELEY

Greeley was the last city in Colorado to have streetcars and one of state's first cities to see the abandonment of its electric car line. From start to finish the Greeley & Denver Railroad Company was in all kinds of trouble.

During the laying of track for the car line, Greeley's first serious labor trouble developed. Some fifty workmen struck for $1.65 a day, twenty cents more than they were being paid. Even though the strike did delay construction some, transit service still got underway in June of 1910.

Service in Greeley started with four second hand cars bought from the city of Spokane. They ran over three and one-half miles of track which formed a convenient city loop. A second line, two miles long, ran out Fourteenth Avenue to Island Grove Park to accommodate rodeo and fair crowds.

There was never an expansion of the original lines but the equipment was up-dated in 1915, with the addition of two new American Car Company cars. These were single-truck, one-man operated, Birney safety cars, painted green and with natural oak interiors.

Two years later disaster struck when the car barns burned to the ground resulting in a $35,000 loss. By then, too, Greeley's love affair with the automobile had begun and the company's revenue was off sharply. Even though maintenance of the line was cut back to the bare minimum and expenses were reduced, there still came a day when there was no money to meet the payroll.

A totally unique plan was then tried. The operators were allowed to pocket whatever five cent fares they could collect just to keep the cars running. Most of their time, one operator recalls, was spent in patching the cars to make them last another day.

The situation went from bad to worse during the early 1920s as the old equipment continued to deteriorate. Finally, only two cars were in service. Then parts from one of them were used to keep the other going. Even it had to be junked in 1923, and the line was dismantled.

Forty-four passenger Denver–built Woeber electric cars were used in Fort
Collins until the city took over the system in 1919. The original big cars were
then junked. (Pioneer Museum, Fort Collins)

In spite of the total destruction of the car, no one was hurt. It collided with a steam
shovel on the Lindenmeier Lake line near the Great Western Sugar Factory.
(Pioneer Museum, Fort Collins)

FORT COLLINS

In a 1947 story about streetcars, **The Saturday Evening Post** **wrote:** "For truly fancy performance in the field of transit, no place on earth can beat Fort Collins, Colorado, smallest town in the United States to boast a trolley system."

Then and until the end, Fort Collins had three street cars running over three single track routes. The little Toonerville Trolley kind of an operation held two pretty impressive distinctions. It had the lowest fares of any transit system in the nation and for some of its years, it made money for the city.

Fort Collins became a "streetcar town" in 1907 when Denver and Interurban Railroad built a short line along College Avenue and out to the resort at Lindenmeier Lake. The company's Fort Collins investment did not pay out and so in 1918, streetcar service was stopped. The following year, the city itself took over the line.

First off, the city junked the big Denver and Interurban cars and put new little Birney cars into service. Then, the Lindenmeier Lake line was discontinued and some four miles of new track relaid. The city operated the system as the Fort Collins Municipal Railway then, for about a third of a century without anymore expansions and with few improvements in rolling stock.

A very personal kind of a transit system, the little cars often stopped at will between regular stops along the city's tree lined avenues to accommodate the people. And while an effort was made to maintain a schedule, one rider recalls how the cars weren't always on time but he allowed it didn't make much difference.

The end came in 1951 after several reprieves. Actually, the line had lost the city money for several years and it was generally known that the cars were not in very good repair. What made it even worse for the old line was an independent bus company's interest in establishing a broad new transit system for the growing city.

But Fort Collins loved her dinky old streetcars and she held on to them just as long as she could. Even when the buses did take to the streets there, it was understood they were simply being "tried."

After the city took over the system, the big cars were replaced with dinky little Birney cars, painted silver and red. They bobbed along over about five miles of tree lined avenues in the northern Colorado city. (Collection of Paul Garde)

Car Number 24 looped through Fort Collins City Park and then returned downtown via Mountain Avenue. The cars ran on a twenty minute schedule. The fare was never more than a nickel. (Collection of Paul Garde)

Fort Collins Municipal Railway solved its safety, switching and transfer problems with an ingenious stunt. Every twenty minutes, all three of the cars met on a wye in a downtown location. (Denver Public Library Western Collection)

Before the automobile drove the streetcar off Colorado's streets and into retirement there were any number of direct encounters. This one took place in Fort Collins.

Colorado's last streetcars operated in Fort Collins. The much loved little line folded in 1951. (Denver Public Library Western Collection)

After abandonment of the Fort Collins system, the little cars were quickly bought up by museums and collectors. Here, Car 25 is on its way to a new home in Victor, Colorado. Others went to the Henry Ford Museum in Detroit and the Colorado Railroad Museum in Golden. One is at the Pioneer Museum in Fort Collins and another is at Pioneer Village, Minden, Nebraska. (Collection of Paul Garde)

BOULDER

Boulder, it seems, wasn't quite ready for the horsecar street railway that started to operate there in 1891. For less than two years later, the horses were sold and the rails and cars were junked.

Six years passed before the foothill city had another go with a rapid transit service. This time it was electric. The first line ran from downtown Boulder to the new Chatauqua Park. Service started in June of 1899 just in time for the opening of that year's Chatauqua season.

Early in the new century after the company had weathered several financial storms, expansion did get underway and the system was extended to a total of five miles. Twenty cars were in use. Single fares were ten cents or books good for twenty rides could be bought for $1.25.

The Boulder Street Railway provided the people of that university town with a clean, comfortable and inexpensive way to get around for almost a third of a century. But in 1931 the electric cars were replaced with a fleet of new Mack buses.

Boulder's first electric cars ran from the downtown section to Chatauqua Park in June of 1899. This was one of the first runs of the new system. The photo was made by Joe Sturdivant, famed Boulder photographer and artist, who in 1910, was killed in a local trolley accident. (Railway Exchange Collection)

Boulder electric car and motorless trailer passing over "the big fill" on that tram systems first line. (Allison Chandler Collection)

Sometime during the 1920s, two new Birney cars were purchased for the Boulder Railway. They were in service until abandonment in 1931. (Railway Exchange Collection)

Denver and Interurban electric car arriving in Boulder from the capitol city. The depot was at Twelfth and Pearl. (Denver Public Library Western Collection)

For over eighteen years, (1908-1926) cars of the Denver and Interurban Railroad made fast and frequent trips between Denver, Boulder and El Dorado Springs. Their slogan was, "Along the foothills and into the mountains". (Denver Public Library Western Collection)

Two of Boulder's electric cars on their road to retirement, June 1, 1931. Even during their last years of use, Boulder's streetcars traveled a total of over 150,000 miles. (State Historical Society of Colorado)

These were the jazzy new Mack buses that replaced Boulder's streetcars in 1931. (State Historical Society of Colorado)

TRINIDAD

The Trinidad Electric Railroad Company wasn't very popular with at least some of the city's population. This is from **The Trinidad Chronicle,** April 28, 1904:

. . . "a team hitched to a corner post proceeded to do acrobatic stunts that would be the envy of any circus horse when the first trolley's head light came around the corner. They reared and plunged, tried to climb the pole, rolled their eyes, stood on their ears and did a well defined hootchie-kootchie. The owner, too, was irate and sprung a beautiful flow of cuss words in the direction of the streetcar."

Even so, in the same issue of that paper, there was another story about how the streets were jammed with people out to see the new cars. At the moment they started their first trips into the city, every steam whistle in town sounded.

Twelve miles of track wound through the city and to the coal camps of Cokedale, Sopris and Starkville. Fare to the camps was fifteen cents. Within the city, the fare was only five cents.

All new cars were put into service in 1917. Nine years later, the line was abandoned.

The people of early Trinidad depended on C. P. Treat's horsecar line to get them around town. In this 1883 photograph, two cars are seen crossing the Purgatoire River bridge on Commercial Street. (The Aultman Collection, Trinadad, Colorado)

Commercial Street was still unpaved in this 1907 photograph showing the East & Main Loop car of the Trinidad Electric Railroad. Trinidad, with a population of about 10,000, was then Colorado's fourth largest city. (The Aultman Collection, State Historical Society of Colorado)

Nine years later, Commercial Street had been brick-paved and a traffic cop had been installed at the Main Street intersection. (The Aultman Collection, State Historical Society of Colorado)

48

The Trinidad Electric Railroad car barn stood just west of the city. The building behind the barn housed the plant that generated the power for the electric cars. (The Aultman Collection, State Historical Society of Colorado)

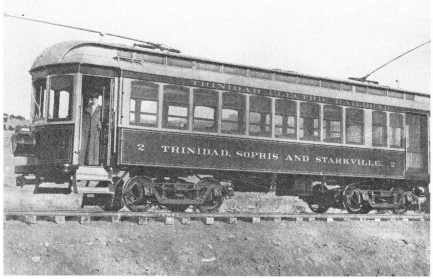

The once busy coal camps of Sopris, Cokedale and Starkville were also served by the Trinidad trolley system. There were two cars to the coal camps every hour, and the fare to them from the city was fifteen cents. (The Aultman Collection, State Historical Society of Colorado)

Grand Junction's first horsecar, 1890. The city took over the line when the company fell behind in its tax and license payments. (Denver Public Library Western Collection)

Grand Junction's Main Avenue in 1909, soon after the electric cars started running there. (Denver Public Library Western Collection)

GRAND JUNCTION

In 1890, the Grand Junction Street Car Company was organized, and for over eleven years it ran two horsecars over one and one-half miles of track on the city's principal·streets. When the company defaulted in their payment of taxes and license fees, the city took it over making it what was probably the nation's first municipally owned transit system.

Several attempts were made to get some company to build a modern transportation system for the growing city, but it wasn't until 1908 that capital became available and the Grand Junction and Grand River Valley Railway Company was organized. In 1909, their electric cars started rolling over three miles of track within the city. The following year, a sixteen mile interurban line was built to Fruita.

Colorado Springs industrialists, including Spencer Penrose who built the famed Broadmoor Hotel, bought the railroad in 1914, and changed the name to Grand River Valley Railway Company. They operated it until 1926.

In 1928, all streetcar service in the city of Grand Junction was discontinued. But the interurban cars ran to Fruita and back for a few years more.

A "California Car," half open and half closed, at the corner of Fourth Street and Main Avenue in early Grand Junction. (Denver Public Library Western Collection)

This was Grand Junction's Main Avenue in 1925, three years before the street cars stopped running in the western slope city. (State Historical Society of Colorado)

Durango, during the gay nineties, looked very much like a city with its Main Avenue electric car line. (Collection of W. Alva Short, Durango, Colorado)

DURANGO

Travelers were more than surprised when, in 1883, they arrived in little Durango to find horsecars waiting for them at the depot. Fewer than 3,500 people lived there then, and towns that size just didn't have street railway systems.

The one and one-half mile line ran from the depot to the Animas River on Main Avenue. Established in 1883, it was first known as the Durango Suburban Street Railway.

The line was electrified and expanded in 1892 and expanded again in 1904. By then, its electric cars were running over about two and one-half miles of track. The equipment consisted of three closed cars, two open cars and one snow. plow.

Hard times came upon the company in the early 1900s and to keep the little line going, it sold off some of the real estate it owned, a piece at a time. Then, it borrowed money from its stockholders and cancelled all free passes. It was beginning to look hopeless.

In 1919, the company asked the Public Utilities Commission for permission to end streetcar service in Durango. It was granted and in 1920, the cars stopped rolling there.

Durango's colorful open cars provided popular summertime transportation to Brookside Park. (Collection of Elvin T. Cobb, Durango, Colorado)

Double-truck electric cars, Number 7 and Number 8, were put to use in Durango in 1904. They traveled the length of Main from the Denver & Rio Grande depot on Fifth Street to Animas City on Thirty-second street. (R. G. Keegan Collection)

One of Durango's electric cars crossing the Animas River on the Main Avenue stone bridge. The little cars ran on a twenty minute schedule. The fare was five cents. (State Historical Society of Colorado)

LEADVILLE

When Leadville was Colorado's second largest city, it boasted a modest street railway which ran almost the full length of Harrison Avenue and then down Chestnut street. Service on the ill fated little horsecar line started in the early 1880s and continued for only a very few years.

The line was plagued with problems from the start. Service, the people of the city claimed, was much too slow. The big cars were simply too long and heavy for the mules to pull with any speed at all. The president of the Leadville Street Railroad Company admitted this in an 1882 **Daily Herald** interview.

But that wasn't the only problem. At an elevation of 10,152 feet, snow comes early and piles deep. It covered the rails, froze them under and made it next to impossible for even the company's big crew to keep the tracks open. Sleighs were sometimes pressed into service until the spring thaw.

If the Leadville mining boom had continued, the city might have had the "neat and speedy" transportation service the **Daily Herald** wrote about. Plans were indeed underway to buy lighter more modern cars. Horses were going to replace the slower mules and new lines were going to be built on which the horsecars were to run on a regular schedule.

Leadville's ill fated horsecar line ran only a few blocks and a few years. (Drawing by Cripple Creek artist, Charley Frizzell)

ASPEN

For a few short years, during the early part of the 1890's, a little horsecar line operated in Aspen. Only two miles long, the tracks zig-zagged from the Colorado Midland depot at the foot of Hunter Street to the northwest city limits. There were tracks along Mill and Galena Streets and Hyman and Cooper Avenues, forming something of a "loop" in the downtown area.

Two open cars traveled over the city's mini-system adding something of a metropolitan flair to the bustling silver mining town. The system was known as The Aspen City Railway.

Aspen's two little horsecars traveled over two miles of track serving a very large part of the city. The system "employed" five horses. (Aspen Historical Society)

Galena Street in 1890 Aspen with one of the horsecars of the Aspen City Railway in the distance. (Collection of James E. Kunkle)

Galena Street 100 years later. (Collection of James E. Kunkle)

ET CETERA

Canon City and Florence came so close to having a trolley system it deserves mention. Had the plan developed, it would have been one of Colorado's most ambitious transportation systems.

The Florence Electric Railway was incorporated at the turn-of-the-century when Florence was a thriving mining, milling and transportation center. The plan was to build an electric car line between Florence and Canon City with a later extension into the Coal Creek and Rockvale coal mining district.

Rolling stock, rail and all the necessary electrical gear was ordered and construction began in 1901. Several blocks of track were laid along Florence's Main and Second Streets. Then, some of the promised financial backing was withdrawn and the project collapsed.

Other Colorado communities for which streetcar systems were planned include La Junta, Gunnison, Montrose, Monte Vista, and even little Palmer Lake.

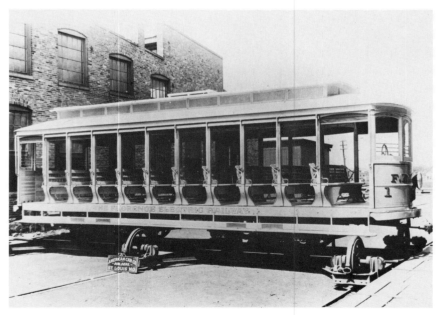

This is one of the cars built by the American Car Company of St. Louis for The Florence Electric Railway. The Colorado company collapsed after a few blocks of track were laid and the cars were never put to use there.

ACKNOWLEDGEMENTS

Wherever I went looking for photos or information about Colorado's old trolley systems I found wonderfully warm and interested people who were anxious to help me. Just having had the pleasure of spending time with all these nice people has made this booklet a very rewarding project for me.

Kay DeFries and Brenda Hawley, Penrose Public Library, Colorado Springs
Rhoda Wilcox, Colorado Springs
Rose Weber, Colorado Springs
Jim Davis, Opal Harber, and Mary Hanley, Denver Public Library
Ralph Peters, Boulder
Kathy Gemeinhardt, Boulder Daily Camera, Boulder
Robert W. Richardson, Colorado Railroad Museum, Golden
Florence Clark, Municipal Museum, Greeley
Alice Gay and Teresa O'Brien, Leadville
Sally Ann Scanlon, The Healey House, Leadville
Al Look, Grand Junction
Marion Fletcher, The Daily Sentinel, Grand Junction
Logan C. Ragle, Southern Colorado Power Co., Pueblo
Marion Murra, Pueblo Regional Library, Pueblo
Ed Gerlits, El Pueblo Museum, Pueblo, Colorado
Elvin T. Cobb, Durango
Sally Morrissey, Durango Herald, Durango
W. Alva Short, Durango
Charles Youngman, Durango Public Library, Durango
Mrs. Walter Wilson and Richard Macomb, Durango
Carl Skaag, Cortez
Arthur Mitchell, Pioneer Museum, Trinidad
G. R. Aultman, Trinidad
Allison Chandler, Salina, Kansas
Mrs. Charles E. Price, Florence
Charles McCandless, Florence
Paul Garde, Colorado Springs
Arthur Anderson, Pioneer Museum, Fort Collins
Ermon Jones, Fort Collins
Morris Cafky, Canon City
James E. Kunkle, Denver

BIBLIOGRAPHY

Ormes, Robert. *Railroads and the Rockies*. Sage Books, 1963.

Jones, Wm. C., Wagner, F. Hol and McKeever, Gene. *Mile-High Trolleys*. National Railway Historical Society, 1965.

Ormes, Manley Dayton and Eleanor R. *The Book of Colorado Springs*. Dentan, 1933.

Taylor, Robert Guilford. *Cripple Creek*. Indiana University, 1966.

Coquoz, Rene. *New Tales of Early Leadville*. 1964

Sarah Platt Decker Chapter of N.S.D.A.R., *Pioneers of the San Juan Country*. Durango Printing Company, 1952.

Sprague, Marshall. *Money Mountain*. Little Brown and Company, 1953.

Hollenback, Frank and Russel, William. *Pikes Peak by Rail*. Sage Books, 1962.

History of the Arkansas Valley. O. L. Baskin & Co., 1881.

Frink, Maurice. *The Boulder Story*. Pruett Press, 1965.

Repplier, F. O. *As A Town Grows*. School District No. 3, Boulder, 1959.

Evans, Dannette. *Spotlight on Pueblo*. 1952.

Everett, George C. *The Cavalcade of Railroads in Central Colorado*. Golden Bell Press, 1966.

Waters, Frank. *Midas of the Rockies*. Sage Books, 1949.

Poors Manuals of Railroads.

Schoolland, J. B. *Boulder, Then & Now*. Pruett Press, 1967.

American Railroad Journal. Golden West Books, 1965.

Lemassena, R. A. *Colorado's Mountain Railroads V*. The Smoking Stack Press, 1968.